Introduction

Suddenly there was a noise behind him again. It wasn't the wind and it wasn't an animal. It was the noise of a man – an angry man.

Paxton looked behind him. Again, no man was there. But wait! Did a shadow move? Paxton didn't know, but he was suddenly very afraid.

Where does the shadow come from? What does it want from Paxton? What is the crown, and why is it important for England?

In M. R. James's famous story, the answers are all in Seaburgh, a small English town near the sea.

M. R. James (1862–1936) was not only a writer. He was a teacher in Cambridge for many years, too. Now he is famous for his short stories. Many of them are about very English places – quiet beaches, small churches, gardens in the sun. But don't read James's stories in the dark!

077146

F. ESOL 3

The Crown

M. R. JAMES

Level 1

Retold by Paul Shipton
Series Editors: Andy Hopkins and Jocelyn Potter

Pearson Education Limited
Edinburgh Gate, Harlow,
Essex CM20 2JE, England
and Associated Companies throughout the world.

ISBN 0582 505410

This edition first published by Penguin Books 2002

1 3 5 7 9 10 8 6 4 2

Text copyright © Penguin Books 2002
Illustrations copyright © Sharp McCaig (Virgil Pomfret) 2002

Typeset by Pantek Arts Ltd, Maidstone, Kent
Set in 12/14pt Bembo
Printed and bound in Demark by Norhaven A/S, Viborg

Published by Pearson Education Limited in association with
Penguin Books Ltd, both companies being subsidiaries of Pearson Plc

For a complete list of the titles available in the Penguin Readers series please write to your
local Pearson Education office or to: Marketing Department, Penguin Longman Publishing,
80 Strand, London, WC2R 0RL.

Chapter 1   Paxton's Story

It's a cold night. Come in and sit down.

Don't be afraid. That noise is only the wind in the trees. Please listen to my story.

It started on a dark, dark night in Seaburgh. Do you know Seaburgh? It's a small English town near the sea. There's a train station near it, and there are some houses and shops. There's one small hotel. The beach is good and long, but the sea is usually very cold. (That isn't a problem for me. I don't like swimming!)

I was at the hotel there with my friend, Henry Long. It was cold that April and there weren't many people in Seaburgh. That was good for us because it was quiet.

It was a good holiday. Every day Long and I walked near the sea. In the evenings we liked to sit in the hotel and talk.

Suddenly, one evening, there was a noise at the door. A young man opened it.

'I'm sorry,' he said to us. 'Please excuse me.'

'That's OK,' I said.

'Come in,' Long said.

The young man came into the light. He was short and he had dark hair. I looked at his unhappy face.

'What's wrong?' I asked. 'Are you OK?'

'Do you want to see a doctor?' Long asked.

'No, no,' the young man said. 'I . . . I'm afraid.'

'Why?' Long asked.

The young man didn't answer my friend's question.

'Sit down and have a drink,' I said. 'What's your name?'

The young man came into the light.

'Paxton.'

He didn't say his first name. (I don't know it today.)

'What's wrong, Paxton?' I asked.

The young man looked at me and then at Long. His eyes were big and his face was white.

'You don't know me,' he said. 'I understand that. But please believe me. Please.'

This was very important to him.

Then Paxton started his story. Long and I listened for a long time. Here is his story.

◆

Paxton was on holiday in Seaburgh, too. He liked old buildings, and there were a lot of them near Seaburgh.

One day he went on his bicycle to a church near the town. It was a beautiful small church.

There was an old picture on it with three crowns. It was very interesting and Paxton wanted to know about it.

There was an old man in the church garden.

'Excuse me,' Paxton said. 'What do you know about this picture?'

The old man put down his spade and looked at the young man.

'Do you know the story of the three crowns?' he asked.

'No,' Paxton answered.

'Seaburgh was always an important place,' the old man said. 'It is today, too. It's important because it's on the sea.'

'I don't understand,' Paxton said.

'The English wanted to protect their country from countries across the sea,' the old man said. 'They put three crowns in the ground near the sea. One of the crowns was here, near Seaburgh.'

'But why?' Paxton asked. He didn't understand. 'What did three crowns in the ground do?'

'The three crowns were magic,' the old man said. 'Their magic protected the country.'

'Do people believe that?' Paxton asked with a smile.

'Many people here in Seaburgh believe it,' the old man answered.

'But do *you* believe it?' Paxton said.

The old man looked at the dark sea. His eyes were dark, too. He didn't answer Paxton's question.

'And where are these crowns now?' Paxton asked.

He looked at the water, too. There was a boat on the sea. It was small on the dark water.

'That's a difficult question,' the old man said. 'One of them is in London now. Every day people on holiday can go and look at it. One of the crowns is in the sea. Now only one crown is in the ground. But its magic is working today.'

'Do you know about the last crown?' Paxton asked. 'Where is it?'

'I don't know that,' the old man said.

'*Who* knows?' Paxton said.

'Only the Agers family.'

'Who are they?'

The old man looked into Paxton's eyes. 'Agers is a very old name in Seaburgh. The Agers were a family here for many years. Families come and go. But the Agers always stayed. They never moved away.'

'And where are these crowns now?'

'Why not?'

'The men of the family had a very important job.' The old man was quiet now. 'The crown protected the country, and the Agers protected the crown.'

Paxton didn't believe the old man's story, but it was very interesting to him.

'Where are the Agers?' he asked. 'Can I talk to them?'

'The Agers can't answer any questions about the crown now,' the old man said. 'William Agers was the last person in the family. He lived near here. But he isn't talking now.'

'Why not?'

Suddenly it was very quiet at the church. The old man put his hand on a gravestone. He looked at Paxton's face. His eyes were cold now.

'You aren't from Seaburgh,' he said. 'Go back to your hotel. Don't think about the crown again.'

'I'm sorry,' Paxton started, 'but ...'

The old man didn't listen. He walked away from Paxton and from the church.

'What did I say?' Paxton asked. Only the wind listened to him.

Then he looked down at the gravestone.

WILLIAM AGERS

This was William Agers's gravestone. The man was dead! Who protected the crown now?

Paxton had many questions, but there were no answers here at the church. It was cold now and the wind was strong. Paxton went back on his bicycle to the town.

The old man walked away from Paxton
and from the church.

He didn't want to think about the crown or William Agers. He stopped at a small shop. There were some old books there. Paxton looked at them because he wanted to read in the hotel that evening.

Suddenly he stopped. The book in his hands was old and black. It was a book for church. There was a name and year in the book: Nathaniel Agers, 1754.

There were a lot of names and years. But the last name was always the same – Agers. This book was in the Agers family for years and years. It went from father to son, from father to son in the family.

Paxton looked at the last name in the book – 'William Agers'. He had William's book in his hands!

'Excuse me,' Paxton said to the tall, thin woman in the shop. 'What do you know about William Agers?'

'That isn't a happy story,' the woman said. 'William Agers is dead. He was young – only twenty-eight.'

'And he didn't have a son?'

'That's right,' the woman answered. 'Mr Agers didn't have a son or a daughter.'

'Where did he live?' Paxton asked. 'I'm an old friend of the family.'

'He lived in a small house near the sea,' the woman said. 'Do you want the address?'

'Yes, please!' Paxton said. He looked for some money in his coat. 'And how much is this book?'

Paxton went to his bicycle again. Later, he arrived at William Agers's small house near the sea. It was dark and quiet there. Behind the house was a hill.

There was a man near the house. 'Can I help you?' he asked Paxton.

Paxton asked the man about William Agers.

'I didn't know him very well,' the man said. 'William Agers was very quiet.'

'Did he have friends?' Paxton asked.

'No,' the man answered. 'Agers didn't like people. He was never in his house. He was always on that hill. He was there in the sun, he was there in the rain. He was there on cold days . . . He was always there.'

'I understand,' Paxton said. The man walked away, but Paxton didn't move.

He looked at the small hill and smiled slowly. Was the last crown there?

◆

It was late now. The room was dark. Long and I looked at Paxton's white face.

'And?' Long said. 'Was it? Was the crown there?'

'Yes, it was,' Paxton answered. 'But it isn't there now.'

'Where is it?' I asked.

'It's in my room.'

I didn't believe him. 'The crown is here in this hotel?' I said.

'Can . . . can we see it?' Long asked.

Paxton didn't answer. We all listened to the wind. Then he said, 'Yes.'

Chapter 2 The Shadow in the Night

Paxton closed the door to his room quickly. Then he put a black bag on the table.

'Is it in there?' I asked.

Paxton didn't answer. Slowly he opened the bag.

In his hand was a black book. It was very old. Paxton opened it for us.

'Can you see the names?' he said.

Long looked at the names in the book. 'William Agers,' he said.

But I didn't look at it. No, I looked at the crown in our new friend's hands. It was very old, but it was beautiful.

I had a lot of questions. How old was the crown? Was it light or heavy? I moved my hand to the crown, but Paxton shouted, 'No!'

I stopped asking questions and looked at Paxton.

'I'm sorry,' he said to me. 'But you don't understand my problem ... I want to put the crown back in the ground.'

I didn't believe him. 'You can't put it back!' I said. 'This crown is very important. Telephone the newspapers in London ...'

'No, you don't understand,' Paxton said again. His eyes were big and afraid.

'OK, let's go to our room,' Long said. 'We can talk about the problem there.'

Paxton put the crown back in the black bag. He went to the door, but then he stopped.

'Wait! Go before me and look in your room,' he said. 'Please!'

'But why?' Long said. 'We're the only visitors in this hotel!'

I moved my hand to the crown, but Paxton shouted, 'No!'

But then we remembered the crown in Paxton's black bag. I opened the door and we looked left and right. There was a person near the door to our room. No, it *wasn't* a person. It was a shadow. It moved quickly.

'Who was that?' Long asked. We were in our room now.

'I don't know,' I answered. 'A hotel worker?'

'No, it wasn't a hotel worker,' Paxton said. He finished his story for us.

◆

Paxton went back to the hotel from William Agers's house that afternoon. In his room, he looked at the Agers's book for a long time. Then he closed the book and went down for food. Later, he went back to the room. The book was open at William Agers's name.

Paxton was afraid, but that didn't stop him. He went to the hill again with his spade. It was dark now, but he didn't stop working. Suddenly there was a noise. Was it the wind?

Paxton looked behind him. Was there a man in the trees? A dark shadow? No, of course not!

Paxton started to work again. The spade was heavy now and it was a difficult job. He wanted to sleep, but he wanted to find the crown, too.

And then it was there. The crown! Paxton smiled. He put his hands on it. Suddenly there was a noise behind him again. It wasn't the wind and it wasn't an animal. It was the noise of a man – an angry man.

Suddenly there was a noise behind him again.

Paxton looked behind him. Again, no man was there. But wait! Did a shadow move? Paxton didn't know, but he was suddenly very afraid. He quickly put the crown in his bag and started to go back to the hotel.

But now the shadow was with him. It was always behind him. Paxton looked back and the shadow always moved quickly away. But then it came back. Sometimes it was near him and sometimes it was far away.

Paxton was very afraid. Who – or what – was the shadow? And what did it want from him?

◆

Paxton stopped. 'That's my story,' he said. 'Do you believe me?'

I didn't believe it, but I didn't say that to Paxton.

'*You* believe it,' I answered, 'and that's the important thing.'

But then I remembered the shadow near the door to our hotel room.

'What can I do now?' Paxton asked.

I looked at Long, then at Paxton.

'OK,' I said. 'We're going to help you. We're going to come with you and put the crown back in its place under the ground. Let's go!'

Paxton smiled, but it wasn't a very happy smile. 'Thank you, thank you!' he said. He went to his room.

I looked at the window. It was a dark night. Long and I put on our coats and went to the hotel door. Paxton was there in front of the hotel. He had the black bag and the spade in his hands.

But now the shadow was with him.

It was cold and we walked quickly. We walked near the church. I put my head down and didn't look up. I didn't want to see the gravestone of William Agers that night.

'Are we near the place?' Long asked. (My friend Henry Long likes walking, but he doesn't usually walk very quickly.)

'Yes,' Paxton answered.

Suddenly I looked left.

'What's that?' I said.

'What did you see?' Long asked.

'There's a man. He's watching us from those trees! I know it!'

We looked and looked at the trees. There wasn't a man there now. But I was afraid. What *did* I see? Was it Paxton's shadow? Perhaps his story wasn't wrong . . . I didn't like this.

'Let's be quick,' Paxton said. 'The shadow knows about us. He's watching us.'

We arrived at the hill. Paxton didn't wait. He started to work with the spade. Long and I only watched.

'Can I help now?' I said to Paxton, but he didn't stop.

'This is my job,' he said.

Then he said to us, 'Give it to me.'

We put the bag on the ground near him, but we didn't open it. Paxton did that. I looked at the crown for the last time in Paxton's hands. He finished the job quickly.

'Is it in the ground?' I asked him.

'Yes.'

I looked at the crown for the last time in Paxton's hands.

I smiled, but Paxton didn't smile.

'Let's go back to the hotel,' Long said. 'It's very late and our beds are waiting for us!'

We started to walk down the hill. Suddenly Long said, 'Remember your coat, Paxton! It's up on the hill.'

I looked up the hill behind us. Long was right. Paxton's long, dark coat was there on the ground. But our new friend didn't move.

'What's wrong, Paxton?' I asked.

His face was white. His mouth moved but he didn't talk.

'Are you OK?' Long asked.

'I . . . I didn't bring my coat,' Paxton said. 'It's in my hotel room.'

The dark thing on the hill wasn't his coat! But what was it?

I looked again. It wasn't there now!

We went down the hill very quickly. We didn't talk. We only listened to the noise of the sea.

Sometimes I looked behind us. Was that a shadow behind the trees? Did a shadow move in the church garden? Was there a dark shadow behind the gravestones?

I didn't know, and I didn't want to know. I wanted to be in my bed. No, I wanted to be far away from this cold, dark place. I wanted to be at home.

We arrived at the hotel at twelve o'clock. A hotel worker opened the door for us. He looked at the three of us.

'It's a cold night,' he said.

I was afraid, but I smiled. 'Yes, it is.'

The hotel worker looked up the road behind us.

'Did you meet any people on the road?' he asked.

'No,' Paxton said. 'We were the only people in Seaburgh.'

'But there was a man behind you . . .' the hotel worker said.

Paxton looked back into the night with big eyes. The shadow wasn't there now.

The three of us went to our room. Paxton went to the window.

'It's OK now,' I said to him. 'The crown is in its place again. You're not in danger now.'

Paxton's eyes stayed on the night.

'Perhaps,' he said.

He went to the door. He said, 'Thank you' to Long and me, and then he went to his room.

'Good night,' I said. 'Sleep well.'

Chapter 3   The Dead Man on the Beach

I don't know about Paxton, but sleep didn't come to me for a long time that night. And then I didn't sleep well. It was a long, long night.

I opened my eyes in the morning and went to the window. The sun's light came into the bedroom. It was late. I looked at the trees. It was a beautiful April day.

I washed and went down. Long was in a big chair with his newspaper and some coffee.

'Do you want some food?' he asked.

'Yes!'

A man was at our table. It was Paxton.

'How are you today?' Long asked.

'I'm ... OK,' our friend answered.

'Did you sleep well?' I asked.

'Yes, thank you. I didn't see the ...' He stopped. 'There wasn't a problem all night.'

'Good!' I smiled. 'Long and I are going for a walk this morning. Please come with us.'

'No, thank you,' Paxton answered. 'I want to stay in the hotel this morning. I'm going to write some letters.'

'This afternoon?' Long said.

'Yes, thank you.'

'Good, good! Let's meet at three o'clock,' Long said. 'Come to our room.'

We said goodbye to him.

Long and I had a good morning. Then we had some food in a café in a town near Seaburgh.

'I like this,' Long said. 'We can have a good holiday again.'

'It's two-thirty,' I said. 'We're meeting Paxton at the hotel at three o'clock.'

Paxton was at the hotel. He had a book in his hands and there was a smile on his face.

'Did you have a good morning, Paxton?' I asked.

'Yes, thank you,' he said. 'I did.'

Long and I wanted to wash. Paxton waited for us.

I went down again quickly, but Paxton wasn't there. Only his book was on the chair.

Long came down, too. 'Where's Paxton?' he asked.

'I don't know,' I said. 'Perhaps he's in his room.'

But there was no answer at Paxton's door. We looked in the hotel garden but Paxton wasn't there. I was a little afraid now.

A hotel worker came to us. 'You're here!' she said.

'Yes,' I answered. 'Why did you say that?'

'Mr Paxton isn't here,' she said. 'He wanted to see you and Mr Long. You were in front of the hotel. You shouted to him. He said ... '

'We didn't shout to him. We were in our room!'

We didn't shout to Paxton. Who did? I was very afraid now.

'Paxton!' I said. 'He's in danger!'

In front of the hotel, we looked for our friend.

'I can't see him!' I shouted.

The hotel worker was at the door behind us.

'He went to the beach,' she said. 'He wanted to see you and Mr Long.'

'Thank you!'

Long and I started to run. It was difficult on the beach, but we didn't stop.

'There! I can see him,' Long said.

There was a person on the beach, but he was far away.

We shouted again and again.

'Paxton! Come back, Paxton!'

'We're here!'

But there was a lot of noise from the wind and the sea. Paxton didn't hear us.

'What ... what's he doing?'

'I don't know. I can't see from here.'

'Look at this, Long!' I shouted.

There were footprints on the beach from Paxton's shoes.

'And look at this!'

This was a footprint, too. But it wasn't Paxton's.

'But what's wrong with it?' Long asked.

'This person didn't have shoes,' I said.

'*Was* it a person?' Long said. 'Perhaps it was an animal . . .' The footprint was very thin.

I didn't answer. A name came into my head – William Agers. But William Agers was dead!

'Quick!' I shouted.

We started to run again. Where was Paxton now?

We arrived at a tall old building on the beach. Long and I started to go up it.

'Where is he?' I asked Long.

Long opened his mouth but he didn't answer. There wasn't time. Suddenly there was a noise. It was a person. A shout. But where did it come from?

'Who's that?' I shouted.

We looked down.

'No!' I shouted.

There was a man on the ground. It was our friend Paxton. He didn't move. His dead eyes looked up at us.

I looked at the dark sea.

'Paxton was right,' I said. 'He did it.'

'Who?' Long asked. 'I don't understand.'

'Agers protected the crown. He was dead, but he protected the crown.'

'But how?' Long said.

I had an answer but I didn't want to say it.

'Perhaps it was an animal.'

It was *magic*. Paxton wanted to find us. He went to the old building. He started to run. Suddenly the shadow was there. But now it wasn't only a shadow. It was William Agers and he was angry. Paxton looked into those cold, dead eyes.

And now Paxton was dead, too.

'What now?' I asked.

'There's a police station in town,' Long said.

We walked back on the beach. The footprints weren't there now. They were under the cold waters of the sea.

I don't remember my time at the police station very well. Only questions, questions, questions:

'Why were you on the beach?'

'Who was there?'

'How did you know Paxton?'

'What did you see?'

Long and I answered all of them. Yes, there was a man on the beach with Paxton. No, we didn't know him. He was very far away. Long and I had the same story, and the police believed us.

But we didn't talk to them about the crown — or about William Agers.

◆

Long and I went away from Seaburgh. That was my last visit there. I'm never going to go to Seaburgh again.

And that's my story. You don't believe me! That's OK — I understand. Before this, I didn't believe stories about magic and dead people.

But listen to this, please.

Don't go to the small town of Seaburgh.

And now Paxton was dead, too.

The little church near the sea is beautiful, but don't go near it.

Don't walk up the hill near the sea and don't look for the last crown.

Why? Because a person in Seaburgh is watching and waiting. He's dead, but that doesn't stop him. He has a job. The crown protects England, and he protects the crown.

He is *always* going to protect the crown.

And me? I'm at home again. I see my friend Long sometimes, but we never talk about our holiday in Seaburgh.

I do my job every day and I'm happy. But at night I don't sleep very well.

In my bedroom, in the dark, I close my eyes and listen to the wind.

I see a cold, dark sea. And under a hill the last crown sits and waits.

ACTIVITIES

Chapter 1

Before you read

1 Look at the first picture in the book. Who are these people?
Where are they? What do you think?

2 Find these words in your dictionary. Put them in the
sentences.

*afraid believe church ground help hill last magic
protect put wind*

a The police . . . . . people.

b We get our water from under the . . . .

c There was a noise at the window. I was . . . .

d I was the . . . . . person at the bus stop.

e I was late for school. The teacher didn't . . . . . my story.

f I always go to . . . . . on Sunday.

g The . . . . . is strong today and it's raining.

h She . . . . . your bag in the car yesterday.

i In the famous story of Arthur, Merlin can do . . . . . .

j We walked up the . . . . . and down again.

k Can you . . . . . me with my homework?

3 Find these words in your dictionary.

beach crown gravestone spade

Which thing do you find

a near the sea?

b near a church?

c on a head?

d in a garden?

After you read

4 Why are these things important to the story?

   a a crown   **b** a church   **c** a book   **d** a hill

Chapters 2 and 3

Before you read

5 What are the three men going to do with the crown? Why?

6 Answer the questions. Find the words in *italics* in your dictionary.

   a You are in *danger*. Are you afraid?

   b The town is *far* from your home. Is it near you?

   c There are *footprints* on your floor. Did you wash it?

   d You can see your *shadow*. Is it a very dark night?

   e You *shout* to your friend. Is she standing near you?

After you read

7 How many dead people were there on the beach? Who were they?

8 The crown is in the ground again. Why was William Agers angry? Talk about it.

Writing

9 A year later, a new person finds the crown near Seaburgh. Write this person's story.

10 You are the old man at the church. You want to protect people from the crown and from William Agers. What are you going to do?